Leonard Bernstein

A LERNER BIOGRAPHY

Leonard Bernstein
IN LOVE WITH MUSIC

CAROLINE EVENSEN LAZO

Lerner Publications Company /Minneapolis

To Jean Shaw

Special thanks to Burton Bernstein for his kindness in reviewing the author's original manuscript of this book.

Lerner Publications Company
A division of Lerner Publishing Group
241 First Avenue North
Minneapolis, MN 55401 U.S.A.

Website address: www.lernerbooks.com

Library of Congress Cataloging-in-Publication Data

Lazo, Caroline Evensen.
    Leonard Bernstein : In Love with Music / by Caroline Evensen Lazo.
      p.   cm.
    Includes bibliographical references and index.
      ISBN: 0–8225–0072–8 (lib. bdg. : alk. paper)
      1. Bernstein, Leonard, 1918–1990—Juvenile literature.
    2. Musicians—United States—Biography—Juvenile literature.
    [1. Bernstein, Leonard, 1918–1990. 2. Musicians. 3. Composers.]
    I. Title.
    ML3930.B48 L39 2003
    780'.92—dc21   2001000336

Manufactured in the United States of America
1 2 3 4 5 6 – JR – 08 07 06 05 04 03

Contents

"The conductor must not only make his orchestra play; he must make them want to play. He must exalt them, lift them, start their adrenaline pouring.... And when this happens ... there is a human identity of feeling that has no equal elsewhere. It is the closest thing I know to love itself."

—*Leonard Bernstein*

Leonard Bernstein gained much of his fame while conducting the New York Philharmonic. Above, he is shown with that famed orchestra in 1960.

❧ Introduction ❧

Bold. Brilliant. Passionate. Kind. These are some of the words students often used to describe their favorite teacher and "all-around musician," Leonard Bernstein. Because of his amazing achievements while still in his twenties, critics called him an American *wunderkind* (wonder child).

Although Leonard Bernstein was best known as a conductor, his extraordinary talent spread far beyond the conductor's podium. There was Bernstein the composer, Bernstein the pianist, Bernstein the teacher, Bernstein the author, Bernstein the television personality, and Bernstein the musical apostle of world peace.

Bernstein was only twenty-five years old when Artur Rodzinski, music director of the world-famous New York Philharmonic Orchestra, appointed Bernstein assistant conductor. Like a stand-in for a star, Bernstein knew that the chance of his ever leading the orchestra before an audience in New York's Carnegie Hall could be years away. Established conductors rarely missed a performance, but only a few months after his appointment, against all odds, one conductor did just that.

On the morning of November 14, 1943, Bernstein was told that guest conductor Bruno Walter was ill. Bernstein would conduct the renowned orchestra that night—with no time for rehearsal. He was also reminded that CBS radio

Bernstein in 1944, shortly after his astonishing New York conducting debut

would broadcast the concert across the country. No one had to remind him that he would be the first American-born conductor to lead a major symphony orchestra in the United States. Making history, however, was the last thing on his mind as the big event approached. He just hoped that everything would go well.

He needn't have worried. Bernstein's debut sent shock waves through the music world. Since he didn't use a baton, he conducted with his arms, shoulders, head, and even his knees. He brought the orchestra to life and the audience to its feet. "[They] roared like one giant animal in a zoo," according to his brother, Burton Bernstein. "It was certainly the loudest human sound I had ever heard. . . . Again and again, Lenny came out to bow . . . always flashing that amazing smile."

The orchestra members were equally elated. "It was the most exciting performance of [Robert Schumann's] *Manfred* Overture I had ever played in my life," violinist Jacques Margolies said. "We knew it was the beginning of a great conductor, like the movie *A Star Is Born*."

Critics, too, were stunned by Bernstein's conducting debut. The *New York Times* editorial page proclaimed, "Mr. Bernstein had to have something approaching genius to make full use of his opportunity. . . . It's a good American success story. The warm, friendly triumph of it filled Carnegie Hall and spread over the airwaves."

No one knew, of course, that one day Leonard Bernstein would be called "the most influential musical force of the twentieth century." But at the moment, on that stage, everyone knew that a star had been born.

In the late nineteenth century, many Russian Jews left their homeland to try their luck in America. This photo depicts three Russian Jews from the village of Ushitza, which is near to where Bernstein's parents grew up in the Ukraine.

❦ ONE ❦

Russian Roots

Leonard Bernstein's father, Shmuel Yosef Bernstein, was born on January 5, 1892. He grew up in a shtetl, a small Jewish sector, in Beresdiv in the Russian Ukraine. Studious and deeply religious, Shmuel seemed destined to become a rabbi. Shmuel's parents, Rabbi Yudel Bernstein and Dinah Bernstein, had established a strong work ethic in the family and were highly respected members of their community. Burton Bernstein described his father's background in Beresdiv:

> Some Jews had small farms just outside the shtetl proper. On such a farm . . . Dinah and Yudel Bernstein made a home: a large shack for a house, a barn for a cow and chickens, and an adjacent field big enough to warrant a plow and a workhorse. While Yudel lost himself in his books and prayers, Dinah set to work plowing the field, sowing seed, cooking meals, milking the cow, collecting eggs, and, to bring in a few steady kopecks [pennies], making Sabbath candles for the Jews and round loaves of Russian rye bread for the Gentiles.

Leonard Bernstein's mother, named Charna Resnick at her birth in 1898, was also born and raised in the Russian Ukraine. Although she lived "only a day's walk" from Shmuel Bernstein's home in Beresdiv, the two never met until they moved to America years later.

Charna's family lived in the prosperous town of Shepetovka, where Jews were restricted to a ghetto, because of the anti-Jewish sentiment that existed in Russia. Although her parents, Simcha and Perel Resnick, were poor, they shared a zest for life and loved music and dancing. They were hardworking, too. Simcha worked in a fur-processing factory while Perel created a small business buying and selling dairy products. The Resnicks were not scholarly like the Bernsteins, but they were religious people.

When Charna was born, she seemed destined to look after her younger brother and sister. Her father, like many Russian men at that time, left to find a better life for his family in America. The family would join him as soon as he had made enough money to support them there. Meanwhile, he would rely on family members to assume the added responsibilities at home.

By 1905 Simcha had earned enough money (at five dollars a week) in the textile mills in Lawrence, Massachusetts, to pay for his family's trip to America. Like most emigrants, the Resnick family traveled in the ship's steerage section, the cheapest passenger section. "Once on the open sea, they all wished they had been turned back to Shepetovka," Burton Bernstein wrote. "The waves were quaking mountains, and some people in [the filthy steerage section] were dying." They finally overcame the sea, however, and arrived at Ellis Island, New York, where immigration inspectors checked their health and other records before releasing them to a sponsor—a relative or other responsible person. When they left the island, they had Americanized names: Charna became Jennie, for example, and Perel became Pearl. On his arrival in New York, Simcha's name had been changed to Samuel.

Because of poverty on the farm and increasing anti-Semitism in the Ukraine, Shmuel Bernstein also decided to escape the shtetl for a better life in the United States. Only sixteen years old at the time, he was ripe for recruitment by the Russian army. In 1908 Shmuel fled to America. Getting there was a nightmare, as it had been for the Resnicks. Memories of the filth, spoiled food, bugs, and excrement he encountered onboard ship stayed with him all of his life.

Immigrant ships bound for America were frequently overcrowded and filthy.

More than twelve million people first entered the United States through Ellis Island in New York. Arriving immigrants were questioned by government officials and examined by doctors in the facility pictured above before being allowed into the country.

When he arrived at Ellis Island, Shmuel Yosef Bernstein became Samuel Joseph Bernstein, soon to be known as Sam. His uncle Herschel ("Harry") met him when he arrived in New York and helped him get started in the New World by finding him a job at a fish market in Brooklyn, New York. Sam cleaned fish and learned English at the same time. Following that job, he worked for his uncle Harry who had a barber shop in Hartford, Connecticut, about one hundred miles away. While there, a customer who was a salesman for Frankel & Smith, a beauty supply firm, noticed Sam's dedication to his work. He offered Sam a job in the Boston branch. Sam took advantage of the opportunity, and, with his uncle's best wishes, moved to Boston, Massachusetts.

Jennie, Leonard, and Sam Bernstein in 1921

❧ TWO ❧

At Home in America

While working in Boston, Sam lived in a rooming house in the suburb of Chelsea. One Sunday in the fall of 1916, a fellow boarder invited Sam on a visit to his cousin Jennie Resnick and her family in Lawrence, Massachusetts. Jennie had been working at a textile mill to help her family survive during hard times. She also attended night school. In fact, Jennie was so busy that she hadn't noticed what an attractive woman she had become.

Although Jennie did not pay attention to her good looks, Sam Bernstein did. Jennie, however, had to be encouraged by her mother to take Sam seriously. Finally, she did. They became engaged a few months later, and on October 28, 1917, they were married.

Differences soon developed between the newlyweds. While Sam's consuming ambition, penny-pinching, and preoccupation with religious studies irritated Jennie, Jennie's love of dancing, adventure, and fun were alien to Sam. In 1918 Jennie became pregnant, and the couple's focus happily shifted to the coming birth.

On August 25, 1918, Louis Bernstein (named after Jennie's brother) was born. Sam and Jennie moved in with the Resnicks so Pearl could help with the baby. Because two boys in the same house were named Louis, Sam and Jennie called the baby Leonard to avoid confusion.

The young parents drew closer together as Leonard brought new joy into their lives. They made his future education their top priority and worked harder than ever to make sure Leonard got the best. They showered the child with love and attention, but they worried as well. Even as a toddler, Leonard suffered from asthma and was "occasionally convulsionary," requiring his mother's full-time care.

Jennie loved doting on Leonard, and he became her greatest source of pride. Leonard continued to hold his parents' marriage together. Although they separated twice during Leonard's early years, their shared pride in their son reunited them. As biographer Humphrey Burton noted, they had good reason to be proud of Leonard:

> According to Jennie, everyone loved him. When the Bernsteins [visited] friends in Revere Beach . . . the family called him the Little Old Man, because he was able to talk so fluently when he was only a year and a half old.

Eventually the Bernsteins left the Resnick home and moved to an apartment in the Boston suburb of Allston, the first of many moves around the city. With each advancement at Frankel & Smith, Sam looked for a larger apartment for his family. When he was promoted to manager in 1920, he began to dream about building a house. But Jennie's focus remained firmly fixed on her son.

Jennie often used music to calm Leonard when he was sick, and it enchanted him—even as a toddler. When Leonard cried, the Victrola—the popular record player at that time—

became a pacifier. "He cried a lot," Jennie recalled. "I'd turn on the Victrola and play him a record and he would stop crying, like on a dime."

He loved listening to Jewish cantors (singers of religious music) and to the popular music of the day. Religious music had the biggest impact on him in his childhood, he said. As the records played, Leonard sat by the windowsill, tapping out the rhythm as he watched the passersby. When he started elementary school, however, he showed no obvious musical talent. He did show a love of learning though and praised his early teachers throughout his life. "Everything they taught me was fun to learn," he recalled.

Leonard's love of religious music was nourished on weekends at Temple Mishkan Tefila (Temple of the Dwelling of

Young Bernstein, at approximately age three

*Four-year-old
Bernstein*

Prayer), which the Bernstein family attended regularly. Leonard never forgot hearing the cantor Isadore Glickstein sing the ancient tunes—handed down orally—and lead the musical part of the service. "The organ would start and then the choir would begin with its colors, and I just began to get crazed with the sound of choral music."

The next big event in the Bernstein family was the birth of Shirley Anne on October 23, 1923. (The baby was named after Anne Shirley, Jennie's favorite actress.)

That same year, Sam Bernstein decided to leave Frankel & Smith to form his own company, The Samuel Bernstein Hair Company. It was a risky decision—one not welcomed by Jennie. "It was rough going from the start," she recalled. "His old bosses wanted [Sam] back . . . at triple his salary . . . but no, not Sam. He loved to be on his own."

To Sam, the freedom to begin one's own business was what America was all about. He was also determined to ensure a secure place for his son in the business world. Already he could foresee Leonard's success in the company. With the invention of the permanent wave machine and Sam's exclusive franchise, or right to sell it, his business boomed. Once again he moved his family to a larger home—this time on Schuyler Street in nearby Roxbury.

Downtown Boston in the 1930s

❧ THREE ❧

Words and Music

While living on Schuyler Street, the Bernsteins received a special gift from Aunt Clara, Sam's sister, who had followed him to America in 1911. Clara was moving from Massachusetts to New York, and she decided to dispose of some furniture—including a sofa and a piano. She gave both to her brother's family.

Ten-year-old Leonard was enchanted with the piano the moment he saw it. "The piano, a handsome mahogany affair, was in the hall for ages because no one knew where to put it, and we had to make room for the sofa," Leonard said. "I remember touching [the piano] the day it arrived, just stroking it . . . . I knew, from that moment to this, that music was 'it.' There was no question in my mind that my life was to be about music."

But the very thought of his son becoming a musician distressed Sam Bernstein. Considering Sam's memory of musicians in the Ukraine, however, the elder Bernstein's reaction was not surprising. The only musicians he had ever seen were the klezmorim—fiddlers who roamed the country playing for kopecks at local events. By the 1890s, the nomadic klezmorim were an integral part of the Ukrainian landscape, and their aimless, meager way of life made a lasting impression on Samuel Bernstein. But Sam saw that Lenny's health improved as he started to play the piano. He gained self-confidence and grew tall. Lenny, as he was called all his life, began by picking out popular songs he had heard on the radio. He remembered "Goodnight Sweetheart" in particular. "I didn't know what notes to play in the left hand, so I would just play anything. . . loudly and triumphantly," he recalled.

Sam always screamed, "Stop that . . . piano!" Fortunately Jennie was always there to support and encourage her son. She could never forget her own first love affair with music while following the klezmorim around her hometown in the Ukraine.

When Lenny wasn't playing the piano, he was playing word games with his best friend, Eddie Ryack. Both had learned about ancient Rome at the William Lloyd Garrison School in Roxbury and decided to form their own little "country," headed by two consuls—as in the Roman republic. The two boys created a mythical country called Rybernia, based on a combination of their last names. Other neighborhood boys who shared their love of language were admitted to the secret society, and Shirley became their mascot. Rybernia had its own culture, humor, and language, and anyone who "talked funny" would inspire them to add new words and phrases—sometimes combining Polish sounds with baby talk—always with humor.

The Rybernian family eventually included Burton Bernstein, born on January 31, 1932. By that time, Leonard was a first year student studying poetry at the Boston Latin School, well known for its standards of excellence in education. He suggested that the baby be named Burton "since it went well, alliteratively speaking, with Bernstein." Leonard

From left to right: *Sam, Shirley, Leonard, and Jennie Bernstein, circa 1935*

was anxious to teach his little brother to speak Rybernian.

Rybernia was no brief episode in the lives of the Bernstein children. It created a bond among them that lasted a lifetime. In 1982 Burton wrote about the significance of their special world:

> The essential point of the private world of the kids was that it had to be a private world of the kids, sequestered from the parents. What we three had in fact achieved was the creation of an imaginary counter-family within the real family.

Lenny had no trouble balancing his imaginary world with the real world or his love of music with his growing love of writing. His teachers at Boston Latin nurtured his love for words—their patterns and rhythms. His essays revealed a student excelling well beyond his classmates. One year Lenny wrote an essay about special kinds of friendship among people of the same sex, challenging the eminent psychoanalyst Sigmund Freud in the process:

> Most people have experienced, at some time during their adolescence, the psychological sublimation of consuming friendship. . . . I am referring [to] that companionship which has been so exaggeratively theorized by the doctrinaire Freud as love between two members of one sex. . . . I could enumerate a list of friends who have formed an integral part of my life, and I, to some extent, of theirs. Why should beautiful relationships like these be smutted with talk of abnormality?

Because of the importance Sam Bernstein placed on learning, Lenny continued to get the best education possible. And Lenny never failed to show his gratitude to his father for working so hard to provide it. Lenny was proud of his father's study of and dedication to the Talmud, a collection of Jewish civil and religious law. It had been "his food since he could first read," and he admired his father's belief in education. His father, however, still believed that the study of music was not a "practical" form of education.

Lenny had to plead with his father for piano lessons. Sam finally allowed him to take beginning lessons with Frieda Karp, a neighbor's daughter, for one dollar an hour. A year later, Lenny wanted more advanced instruction and took lessons from Susan Williams at the New England Conservatory of Music. Those lessons cost three dollars an hour (expensive in those days), and Sam was once again enraged. Was his son becoming too interested in music? Was music becoming more than a hobby? Where would these lessons lead his son? Such questions plagued Sam as he once again conjured up memories of the poor Ukrainian klezmorim. Also, Sam believed that "American Jewish boys had no chance in the field of serious music." At the time, America's great conductors and musicians were elderly Europeans.

Sam was proud of his son's achievements, but he worried about Lenny's future. Finally Sam convinced himself that Lenny would tire of the piano and would one day join the Samuel Bernstein Hair Company. Hoping to get music out of his son's system, Sam helped pay for the piano lessons Lenny wanted so desperately. Lenny paid the rest of the cost by forming a small band that played at dances, weddings, and bar mitzvahs (ceremonies that honor the passage of thirteen-year-old Jewish boys into adulthood).

Lenny's own bar mitzvah in 1931 centered around a speech he had written in both English and Hebrew. Sam Bernstein was so proud of his son that he gave him a baby grand piano to replace the upright that Aunt Clara had given the family. Sam even took Lenny to his first concert the

Bar mitzvah is the entry of a Jewish boy into the adult Jewish community. This usually takes place at age thirteen and involves much study, frequently with the aid of parents and community members.

following year—a benefit for Temple Mishkan Tefila by the Boston Pops Orchestra. Soon afterward, a business associate gave Sam two tickets to a piano recital by famed Russian composer, pianist, and conductor Sergey Rachmaninoff at Boston's Symphony Hall, and Sam invited Lenny to go with him. Sam's attendance demonstrated his loyalty to his homeland, his business friend, and his son. "Though Sam suffered through [that concert], I was thrilled to pieces," Lenny said.

Whenever Sam showed the slightest interest in classical music, Lenny showed his gratitude. For example, in a recital for the Brotherhood of the Temple, Lenny played music based on a Hasidic meditation he had heard his father sing. (The term *Hasidic* refers to a popular Jewish religious movement founded in Eastern Europe during the eighteenth century.) Lenny had hoped to please his father by playing something familiar to him and at the same time to relay his own deep love of music. He succeeded in impressing his father and all the other Brotherhood members too.

Lenny impressed his peers as well. When Mildred Spiegel was a sixteen-year-old piano student, she met the fourteen-year-old musician.

> He came after school hours from Boy's Latin to my school, Roxbury Memorial High School for Girls. I found him playing the "Malagueña" by [Cuban composer Ernesto] Lecuona on the Steinway grand in a large empty auditorium surrounded by a small group of admiring students. I was astonished at his sense of drama, verve, authority, [and] stupendous enthusiasm [for the Spanish dance music] . . . . He sounded like an orchestra. It was love at first sight. We fast became musical friends, playing lots of duets [two people playing on one piano] and two pianos almost every Tuesday afternoon, alternating between the Harvard Musical Society and the New England Conservatory of Music, where we would meet under the heroic bronze statue of Beethoven.

Sam's hope that his son would tire of music and "get it out of his system" seemed dimmer than ever. Lenny's commitment to music was growing stronger every day, and by the fall of 1932 he felt ready to audition for Heinrich Gebhard, one of Boston's most esteemed piano teachers. While Gebhard quickly spotted Lenny's innate musical talent, he found him lacking in his attention to technique. He urged Lenny to study with Helen Coates—the best of his assistants. Miss Coates was a brilliant, warm, and loving teacher, and she charged only six dollars per lesson—far less than Gebhard's fifteen-dollar fee. Yet if Lenny decided to study with Miss Coates, Gebhard would occasionally evaluate his progress. Excited about the plan, Lenny presented it to his father.

Sam was unconvinced and refused any more financial help. Lenny paid for his new lessons with the money earned

Miss Helen Coates, shown here later in her life, was one of Bernstein's first piano instructors. She became his personal secretary and confidante.

from his dance-band jobs. Miss Coates was delighted. She understood his commitment to music and recognized his talent instantly. She even scheduled Lenny's lessons at the end of the day so the hour could stretch out longer. "She taught me how not to 'bang,' how to use the pedal discreetly, how to discipline my crazed and raging fingers," Lenny said. Miss Coates also indulged Lenny's fascination with opera, and together they pored over piano scores of the operas he loved. They were as in tune with each other as they were with music.

Both Sam and Jennie were relieved that Lenny never let his schoolwork suffer because of his broadening interest in music. In fact, Lenny continued to rank at the top of his class at the Boston Latin School. His preoccupation with music never weakened his close relationship with his siblings either. Summer activities—especially musical—continued to strengthen their bonds.

Bernstein conducting the Camp Onota Rhythm Band in 1937

❦ FOUR ❦

"Crazy Artist Nuts"

After renting a house in the lakeshore community of Sharon, Massachusetts, for the month of July in 1931, Sam decided to build a summerhouse there. He also built a house in Newton, which in the 1930s was a somewhat rural suburb of Boston. The Newton home became the "family shrine" Sam had always dreamed about. But it was the summers in Sharon that the Bernstein children loved so much—and that almost drove their father crazy.

Twenty-five miles south of Boston, Sharon was one of the few communities that welcomed Jewish residents when anti-Semitism was on the rise, enriching the community in the process. Prejudice against the Jews in the Boston area did not result in the violence that Sam remembered from his experience in Russia, but nevertheless prejudice was alive in the United States in the 1930s. Sharon became more than just a summer home for the Bernsteins. It became a harbor for Lenny's creative friends and a showcase for their talent—with Lenny clearly in charge. Sharon was also the backdrop for Lenny's first romance.

In his early teens, he was smitten with Beatrice Gordon, whose aunt lived near the Bernsteins. Lenny "would spend hours at her house and send her his writings. He signed his poems 'Lamb's Ear' and called Beatrice his 'Rosebeam.'" He also sent her an essay "in which he shows a side of himself that was unusually well hidden. He absolutely had to have people around him, he wrote, as a bulwark against some unbearable feelings of loneliness and severe inner doubts about his future." But Beatrice was not the only girl interested in Lenny. "He was surrounded by girls," his friend Mildred Spiegel said. "Any mother who met him and had a

This collectible opera card depicts a scene from Bizet's Carmen. *Bernstein began his musical career by staging a production of this opera during a family vacation in the summer of 1934.*

daughter would invite him home for dinner."

During the summer of 1934, it seemed that everyone was drawn to Lenny. His production of Bizet's famous opera *Carmen* involved family and friends alike. Burton Bernstein described the production: "Since most of the people we could find for the chorus were girls, we had what turned out to be an all-male chorus sung by females, costumed as little old men wearing yarmulkes [skullcaps] . . . and the wigs were supplied by none other than the Samuel Bernstein Hair Company. . . . Shirley, who was just nine years old and had some teeth missing . . . spoke the prologue."

Carmen was staged in the dining room at Singer's Inn, a resort hotel in Sharon, and the whole summer colony came to see it. Few would ever forget seeing young Leonard Bernstein "in black wig and mantilla, alternately playing the piano and singing *Carmen.*"

Jennie was, as always, Lenny's biggest fan and loved the production. Sam was pleased that his wigs—as well as his son—were such a success. But he believed that such events were just summer fun and not the stuff of a profitable career for his son. Sam also hoped that Lenny would become too absorbed in academic pursuits to mount more shows and that the Sharon house would become the peaceful place he had always dreamed it would be.

In 1935 Lenny graduated from the Boston Latin School with many prizes and honors to his credit—including the class song. "[It] was the first completed work that I ever wrote down," Lenny said. At the Class Day exercises, Lenny played a piano duet with Edward Goldman, a fellow student, and accompanied violist Jerome Lipson (who later became a member of the Boston Symphony Orchestra).

A diploma from Boston Latin was held in high regard by

Bernstein attended the prestigious Boston Latin School for his high school education. This plaque can still be seen at the school.

colleges—not only because of the school's quality education but also because of its history. Built in 1635, the school's illustrious past pupils included Benjamin Franklin, Samuel Adams, John Quincy Adams, John Hancock, and Ralph Waldo Emerson. For Sam and Jennie Bernstein, immigrants from Russia, Lenny's graduation from such a prestigious school was a monumental honor—and a springboard, they hoped, to Harvard University in nearby Cambridge. "With the fine recommendations I have received," Lenny told Helen Coates, "I should be accepted into Harvard." And he was.

Although Sam was adamant about a "practical" course of study for his son—something that would prepare him for the business world—Lenny chose music for his major at Harvard. Sam finally relented and reluctantly accepted his choice, but he would not agree to pay for advanced piano instruction from Heinrich Gebhard. Once again, Lenny prevailed by paying for his lessons out of his income from dance-band jobs. He also earned money from teaching beginning piano students in Boston. His tight schedule never kept him from breaking loose in the summer, however. Lenny's friends could hardly wait to join him in Sharon to provide the community with more rousing musical shows. Not surprisingly, Sam did not share their enthusiasm. To him they were all "crazy artist nuts."

In July 1935, Lenny and his friends presented the Sharon community with their production of Gilbert and Sullivan's operetta *The Mikado,* featuring Lenny's eleven-year-old sister, Shirley, and other local talent. They formed the Sharon Community Players and staged the operetta at the Sharon Town Hall auditorium. Lenny directed the work, selected the props and scenery, and sang the leading role. "Bernstein

The lead roles in Gilbert and Sullivan's operetta The Mikado *are challenging for professional singers,* left, *but Bernstein was ambitious enough to stage this show with family and friends in 1935.*

[was] always center of the crowd," according to Victor Alpert, one of the players. "[His] personality was so strong that there was no question who was the leader of the gang." Shirley Bernstein recalled the rehearsals in the Sharon house: "Strewn around our living room were thirty-odd young performers draped carelessly over the furniture and sprawled on the floor, singing away at the top of their voices to Lenny's direction." Jennie Bernstein was not pleased when Lenny snagged her maid for a leading role and carted her off to the auditorium in Jennie's car—leaving housework undone and no car to drive! Yet she remained an adoring mother.

One of the players suffered an appendectomy and was unable to perform. She described Lenny's special way of lifting her sprits while she recuperated:

> Lenny came over, and sitting at the piano, played and sang the entire score of *The Mikado* and acted out each part. He was wonderful. With all the concerts I've seen him do on TV since, I have never got a greater bang out of anything than that impromptu performance.

For Burton Bernstein, too, *The Mikado* was unforgettable. Only three years old at the time, he enjoyed "the frenetic scene" in the Sharon house during rehearsals of the operetta. "I have been told that I learned by rote practically the entire score . . . while I was supposed to be having my afternoon naps."

Buoyed by his success in Sharon that summer, Lenny embarked on *H.M.S. Pinafore* the next year. The more experience he got, the more confidence he gained. In 1937, while he was a counselor at Camp Onota in Pittsfield, Massachusetts, he launched *The Pirates of Penzance*—another popular Gilbert and Sullivan operetta. Adolph Green, a talented young man from New York, starred as the Pirate King. Lenny admired Green's knowledge of music and loved his sense of humor. The two became close friends.

When Green was a guest at the Bernstein home in Sharon, however, his musical virtuosity and sense of humor totally escaped Lenny's father. "When Lenny invited Green to Sharon," Burton Bernstein noted, "they would sit around the house for hours, quizzing each other on, say, Beethoven scherzi [short, lively musical compositions] and inventing brilliant musical parodies while Sam stewed and paced. 'Who is that nut?' he'd say." Eventually both Sam and Jennie grew fond of Green.

Bernstein at the piano, 1936

❧ FIVE ❧

On, Chopin! On, Schubert! On, Copland and Blitzstein!

Although Harvard and Boston Latin School were only minutes away from each other, their attitudes and rules regarding minorities were light-years apart. Admission to Boston Latin was based solely on academic merit. One's race or religion played no role in being accepted there. Not so at Harvard. At that time a racial quota was in effect, and not more than 10 percent of Harvard's students could be Jewish. Inclusion in that select 10 percent, however, did not guarantee freedom from prejudice. In fact, Lenny was excluded from several clubs and never invited to perform with the Hasty Pudding Show, well known for its musical satires. But Lenny seemed too busy to worry about the anti-Semitic snubs. He was preoccupied with his academic courses, piano classes with Heinrich Gebhard in Boston, and his athletic activities. He loved to play squash in winter and row on the Charles River in spring.

43

Lenny's freshman courses at Harvard included English literature, fine arts, Italian, and German. He studied music with Professor Arthur Tillman Merritt. Together they would play the music of Claudio Monteverdi as recommended by Merritt's French teacher, the renowned Nadia Boulanger. Lenny later wrote, "We would sit and play and sing with joy. . . . I will never forget the first time we sang *Orfeo* and played it four hands together!"

Seventeen-year-old Lenny was handsome with dark wavy hair and hazel eyes. He was, despite his history of asthma, rarely without a cigarette in his hand. (The dangers of smoking were not known in the late 1930s, and the habit was a popular one.) His magnetic personality attracted people in droves. According to Mildred Spiegel, "he was . . . outgoing, fun-loving, surrounded . . . with many friends and had an abundance of acquaintances from all walks of life." She noted that his enthusiasm was "contagious." Another classmate, William A. Whitcraft Jr., played piano duets with Lenny in the Eliot House (dormitory) common room. "While Lenny coached me in Bach . . . I exposed him to boogie-woogie," he remembered. "I must say, he absorbed any and all kinds of music and was instantly able to repeat anything I played."

Lenny continued to explore the music of great composers, ranging from Frédéric Chopin and Franz Schubert to Aaron Copland, Marc Blitzstein, and many others, spanning approximately 150 years of classical music. He loved it all. He believed that if one loved life, one loved music (or could learn to love it). To Lenny, life and music were inseparable. Pablo Picasso, the titan of twentieth-century art, felt the same way about art. When someone once asked him, "What is art?" Picasso replied, "What is not?" If the question had been posed to Lenny about music, his answer surely would have been the

Bernstein's striking good looks and charming personality made him popular with his Harvard classmates.

same. "Life without music is unthinkable," he said. "Music without life is academic. That is why my contact with music is a total embrace."

Given the choice, Edwin Geller no doubt would have picked a visual artist for a roommate at Harvard instead of a musical one. He had "devoutly hoped for" a "quiet" roommate. When he saw workers carrying a piano up the stairs and into the bedroom next to his, such hopes were dashed. Then he learned that Bernstein was moving in. "It would do no good to complain," Geller said. "Everyone thought he was a genius and recognized it. . . . There was nothing he couldn't play. . . popular, Gilbert and Sullivan, jazz, the classics—he could do it all."

Along with his upright piano, Lenny brought an impressive repertoire of classical music to Harvard, including Prelude and Fugue in F Minor by Johann Sebastian Bach; the

Sonata in D Minor by Ludwig van Beethoven; Rhapsody in G
Minor by Johannes Brahms; the *Novelette* in E Major by
William Schuman; the *Sequidilla* by Isaac Albéniz; *The Juggler*
by Ernst Toch; *Danse Nègre* by Cyril Scott; *La Cathédrale en-
gloutie* and *Poissons d'or* by Claude Debussy; *Cracovienne fantastique* by Ignacy Paderewski; many Chopin nocturnes,
rondos, polonaises, and preludes; and works by Edvard Grieg
and Franz Liszt.

Lenny credited Heinrich Gebhard for improving his tone
and polishing his playing. When he played Ravel's Concerto
in G Major with the Massachusetts State Symphony, conducted by Alexander Thiede, the *Christian Science Monitor*
critic wrote: "Bernstein possesses unlimited technique.
Although still in his teens, he plays with an authority and ease

*This photograph shows a view of Lowell and Dunster dormitories
at Harvard University in 1930. Bernstein studied music at
Harvard during the 1930s.*

which betoken an unusual talent. His tone is crisp, and his finger work clean and clear cut."

Music involved adventure as well as hard work for Lenny. One of his favorite off-campus hangouts was Briggs & Briggs, a music store in Boston, where he listened to new recordings. When he discovered a recording of Piano Variations by Aaron Copland, an idol of his, Lenny "went crazy." Unable to afford the sheet music, he went to his philosophy professor, David Prall, who bought it for him. In turn, Lenny wrote a paper on the composition for Prall's aesthetics class. The more Lenny thought about Copland's music, the more he dreamed about playing duets with the master.

"The Piano Variations had virtually become my trademark," Lenny said. "I was crazy about them—and I still find them marvelous today—but in those days I especially enjoyed disrupting parties with [the harsh and dissonant sounds]. . . . I could be relied upon to empty any room in Boston within three minutes by sitting down at the piano and starting it."

Whenever possible, Lenny attended concerts by the Boston Symphony Orchestra conducted by Serge Koussevitzky, another of his idols. In January 1937, a guest conductor named Dimitri Mitropoulos, who had made his debut with the orchestra the year before, returned for a performance that Lenny attended. He was thrilled by Mitropoulos's dramatic style and power and said he "had gone bananas" over it.

The next day, he attended a reception for the conductor and was asked to play for him. Lenny played a sonata that he had written for Heinrich Gebhard. Mitropoulos was so impressed that he invited Lenny to come to his rehearsals for upcoming concerts with the Boston Symphony.

Lenny skipped classes for almost a week to learn as much from Mitropoulos as possible. He was especially moved by the orchestra's performance of Robert Schumann's Second Symphony.

Mitropoulos called Bernstein a young genius and urged him to focus all his time on music. He was convinced that Lenny showed signs of greatness. No one that famous had ever praised Lenny so highly or raised his hopes as Mitropoulos had. A few years later, when Mitropoulos became conductor of the Minneapolis Symphony Orchestra, he urged Lenny to concentrate on conducting instead of composing and hoped he would become his assistant conductor. Because he was still a student and not a resident of Minnesota, however, Lenny could not qualify for that post. "Our loss was the world's gain," former Minneapolis Symphony patron Peter Evensen said.

In his junior year at Harvard, Lenny's love of music continued to lure him away from his other studies. Yet he managed to get an A in English and a B in literature. Hard-working students like Harold Shapero were struck by Lenny's ability to get good grades without studying or even appearing in class sometimes. Others were put off by his cavalier attitude and called him a show-off. Ironically, the lowest grade he received that year was in music. Professor Merritt gave him a C. "I never graded students on their talent," he said. "If he didn't do the work why should I give him an A? That was my theory, and [it] applied to all my students . . . so I gave him a C."

Such grades did not deter Lenny from pursuing his musical activities beyond the Harvard campus. His friend and fellow student I. B. Cohen shared his interests. On November 14, 1937, Lenny joined Cohen at the New York debut recital

*Conductor Dimitri
Mitropoulos*

of Anna Sokolow, a member of Martha Graham's dance company. They got tickets through Cohen's friend, poet Muriel Rukeyser. The three sat together in the balcony of the Guild Theater for the recital. After taking his seat, Lenny noticed the man seated next to him:

> Already in his seat on my right was an odd-looking man in his thirties, a pair of glasses resting on his great hooked nose and a mouth filled with teeth flashing a wide grin at Muriel. She leaned across to greet him, then introduced us: "Aaron Copland . . . Lenny Bernstein." I almost fell out of the balcony.

After the dance recital, Copland invited Lenny to join some friends at his loft for a birthday celebration. Being included in the special party ("with artists!" he said) excited Lenny, and he couldn't wait to play the Variations as his gift to Copland. He played the master's work with such conviction that Copland commented, "I wish I could play it like that." From then on, they were friends.

Lenny studied advanced harmony and the fugue with Walter Piston and orchestration with Edward Burlingame Hill at Harvard, but he learned composition from Copland during subsequent visits to New York. Copland gave Lenny blunt but constructive criticism. Lenny said, "I would show Aaron bits and pieces [of works written at Harvard]. . . and he would say, 'All that has to go. . . . You've got to start fresh. . . take these two bars and start from there.'. . . He taught me about. . . style and consistency in music. . . . Then would come that glorious day when. . . we would play four hands." They played Copland's *Billy the Kid, Outdoor Overture*, Piano Sonata, and Third Symphony long before they were played for the public. Lenny received advice as well as instruction from Copland. "It was always Aaron to whom I would turn with my worries," he said.

During his last two years in college, Lenny threw himself into several activities. He became a writer for the *Harvard Advocate,* and he wrote reviews for New York's *Modern Music.* He reviewed Sergey Prokofiev's First Piano Concerto, conducted by the composer himself, with typical chutzpah (extreme self-confidence): "Truthfully," Lenny wrote, "it is not a good piece . . . its one real tune is worked to death . . . it lacks continuity, and it sounded like a student work that it is." That from a young Harvard student!

Lenny considered himself an active citizen as well as a student. Social issues were important to him—especially those that involved prejudice against minorities and oppression of the weak by the strong. "At Harvard," he wrote, "we had all-night bull sessions; we marched, we demonstrated; I played the piano for strikers, for Spain, for blacks, for one cause after the other. And none of this seemed to conflict with my studies, whether musical or literary or philosophical; it all blended together . . . I felt myself a young artist and a young citizen."

Leonard Bernstein and Aaron Copland were intimate partners as well as trusted musical advisers to one another.

Lenny was especially aroused by Marc Blitzstein's satirical opera *The Cradle Will Rock*. The one-act opera, concerning a steelworkers' strike against a powerful steel-mill owner, had been a big hit in New York. To Lenny, the issue of injustice in the workplace was well worth dramatizing, and he couldn't wait to direct the opera in Cambridge. In 1939, with Marc Blitzstein's blessing, Lenny launched the awesome task of finding both the funds and the talent to make *The Cradle* rock at Harvard.

Bernstein gave this Harvard graduation portrait to his teacher and friend Helen Coates in 1939.

❧ SIX ❧

Signs of Greatness

Often do the spirits
of great events stride on
before the events
And in today already walks
tomorrow.

—Samuel Taylor Coleridge

With less than two weeks to rehearse *The Cradle Will Rock*—and no money to pay for the production—Lenny enlisted the help of fellow student Harold Williams. Williams had a strong initial reaction to the proposed project:

> When Lenny first gave me the play to read, I thought it was pure trash and wanted nothing to do with it. [He] asked me to withhold judgment until I could hear the music.... Then he ... played the score through, singing each part himself. I was sold, and I agreed to handle all the business aspects of the production ... Lenny would do the direction and play the piano.

Patrons, including professors Arthur Schlesinger and David Prall and poet-playwright Archibald MacLeish, were quick to fund the production. Lenny even talked his parents into letting fifteen-year-old Shirley (then a student at Newton High School) play a prostitute in the opera. "At the supper table before she set off [for rehearsals] her father would say gloomily that he hoped the police would catch her driving underage without a license."

Conservative political groups had labeled the New York production of *Cradle* left-wing propaganda because of its workers' rights theme, but it still won high praise. The Harvard production was applauded instantly. According to Elliot Norton, drama critic of the Boston *Post*, it featured "the most talented student cast this department has ever seen." And Marc Blitzstein, the master behind *The Cradle Will Rock,* raved about Shirley Bernstein's performance. In general, critics praised the Harvard production under Lenny's direction for its energy, passion, and wit—three chief characteristics of the director himself.

Lenny had also composed and conducted music for *The Birds* by fifth-century B.C. Greek playwright Aristophanes. Although the music was mainly a collection of short pieces for a small orchestra, the production marked Lenny's first appearance on the podium.

All across the Harvard campus and in music circles around Boston, Leonard Bernstein had become known as an exceptional talent. As a composer, conductor, pianist, and writer, he could, as his roommate had said, "do it all." Marc Blitzstein had recognized Lenny's musical gifts soon after meeting him. He also saw in him a kindred spirit. Blitzstein said:

> We are . . . . musical brothers . . . . I remember one day we were lying on the banks of the Charles River,

looking up at the sky. Lenny was saying he didn't know *what* to be [after his graduation]. He had . . . no sense of limitation . . . one didn't know from which springboard he would dive, but we knew there would be a hell of a splash.

As graduation approached, Lenny worried about his ability to earn a living in the field of music. Was his father right? Would it be impossible for a young American Jewish boy to find a job in the world of classical music? Would he have to sell beauty supplies for his father instead?

In June 1939, Lenny graduated *cum laude* (with distinction) from Harvard. His friends thought *magna cum laude* (with great distinction) would have been more appropriate. To Lenny's parents, however, any degree from Harvard was a high honor, and they were thrilled with their son's achievement. As for Lenny, he was happy to have Harvard behind him so he could get on with his life—in music, he hoped.

Bernstein graduated from Harvard University in June 1939.

After graduation Sam urged Lenny to take a guaranteed, full-time job with the family company. As usual, Lenny had something else on his mind—a visit to New York where his old friend Adolph Green lived and worked. First Lenny had to persuade his father to agree. Sam was sure Lenny would be unable to break into the classical music scene in New York. Banking on that hunch, Sam gave Lenny enough money to spend the summer in New York with Adolph. The tiresome task of job hunting would get to him eventually, Sam hoped, and would prompt him to return home.

Adolph Green had joined a group of entertainers called the Revuers, who staged small nightclub acts in New York. Occasionally Lenny provided piano accompaniment for their acts. To qualify for a permanent job in the music field, Lenny would have to live in New York for six months and join the musicians' union. So when the summer ended, he returned to Boston. Before he left, he bought a clarinet in a pawnshop for four dollars. Playing the instrument gave him comfort as he faced the reality of leaving New York.

On his return to Boston, his spirits were lifted when a friend told him that Dimitri Mitropoulos had called and wanted to see him. He went back to New York to meet with the master whose praise had encouraged him so much. Once again Mitropoulos heaped praise on Lenny and convinced him that he should concentrate on conducting. Recalling that pivotal meeting, Lenny said, "I had never entertained the notion of being a conductor; that was a brand new idea which had just that summer been instilled in my brain by Dimitri Mitropoulos."

Mitropoulos advised him to study conducting at the Curtis Institute in Philadelphia, Pennsylvania, where the esteemed conductor Fritz Reiner taught. After Lenny auditioned for Reiner, he was not only admitted to Curtis but was also awarded

Conductor Fritz Reiner worked with Bernstein at the Curtis Institute in Philadelphia.

a scholarship. Sam pitched in with some living expenses—never giving up hope that his son would one day get music out of his system and want to work in the family business.

Curtis Institute was not known for its fun-filled times. The teachers were demanding and deadly serious. The two-year program included conducting (with Reiner), orchestration (with Randall Thompson), and piano (with Isabelle Vengerova). Madame Vengerova taught piano the Russian way. She was "dogmatic . . . about hand position . . . and extremely slow practicing, hands separately, with accents every few notes," pianist Gary Graffman wrote. She often terrified students with screams and threats. She "was extremely wide, and she sailed around her studio like an overstuffed battleship in search of the enemy, cannon loaded and ready to fire." Madame Vengerova was a far cry from the quiet and graceful Helen Coates or the dignified Heinrich Gebhard. Still, to Lenny, Madame Vengerova was at once "tyrannical and brutal and fabulous. . . . She taught me how to listen to myself, which is the greatest gift any teacher can give a student."

Fritz Reiner was demanding, too. Lenny paid close attention to his teaching in particular. After all, it was Reiner's knowledge of conducting that Lenny was primarily interested in.

Lenny had expected his future as a conductor to begin with Mitropoulos and the Minneapolis Symphony. He had never given up hope that he would become the maestro's assistant conductor, but once again that opportunity failed to materialize. At the end of his first year at Curtis, he returned home for the summer of 1940.

With recommendations from conductors Reiner and Mitropoulos and distinguished composers Aaron Copland, Roy Harris, and William Schuman, Lenny auditioned for Serge Koussevitzky in hopes of attending the maestro's new music school, the Berkshire Music Center, later to be called the Tanglewood Music Center. The Center is nestled in the Berkshire Mountains in northwestern Massachusetts, and is the summer home of the Boston Symphony Orchestra.

Surrounded by spacious lawns, trees, gardens, and views of Lake Mahkeenac, Lenny thought Tanglewood would be the ideal place to nurture his love of music. When he was accepted as one of Koussevitzky's three student conductors, Lenny was ecstatic. In his first letter from Tanglewood to his brother Burton, Lenny wrote:

> I have never seen such a beautiful setup in my life. [Koussevitzky] is the most marvelous man—a beautiful spirit that never lags or fails—that inspires me terrifically. And he told me he is convinced that I have a wonderful gift [and] is already making me a *great* conductor. . . . I am so thrilled. . . . The orchestra. . . responds so beautifully in rehearsal. Of course the concert tomorrow night (Shabbas yet!) will tell

whether I can keep my head in performance. . . if it goes well, there's no telling what may happen.

Critics from both Massachusetts and New York praised the concert—in which Bernstein conducted Randall Thompson's Second Symphony. "His talent was obvious," the *Boston Evening Transcript* reported, and "his musical intentions were correct and inspiring." Lenny credited Koussevitzky for teaching him an invaluable lesson: "Between one beat and the next you *prepare*. . . . [The secret] is what is *between* the beats; it is the inner beats that are important."

In addition to Koussevitzky, the Tanglewood faculty included Lenny's idol Aaron Copland, British composer Paul Hindemith, and Russian-born cellist Gregor Piatigorsky, among others. Studying with such extraordinary teachers in

Aaron Copland, Bernstein's friend and mentor, was one of the faculty members at Tanglewood during Bernstein's time there.

such an idyllic environment was every music student's dream come true. Lenny was one of 312 students at Tanglewood. He paid the tuition with money earned from his work with the Revuers in New York and a fifty-dollar scholarship.

Lenny's joyful spirit attracted many friends. Vera Tilson had vivid memories of Lenny at Tanglewood:

> He was so magnetic, and the center of attention wherever he went.... We went on outings into the countryside. Once we passed a playground full of children and Lenny insisted on stopping and talking to the kids. He immediately began organizing them into group games, just like a camp counselor. The remarkable thing is that they did exactly what he told them. He was hypnotic.

Bernstein steps from the podium after conducting at Tanglewood.

Conductor and Tanglewood instructor Serge Koussevitzky had a profound influence on Bernstein's life and career.

His fun-loving spirit attracted one woman in particular—Jacqueline ("Kiki") Speyer, daughter of Louis Speyer, who played the English horn with the Boston Symphony. Although Kiki and Lenny cared about each other—and even thought about getting married someday—the relationship did not work out. Harold Shapero, Lenny's roommate at Tanglewood, claimed that students were too busy making music to become deeply involved in relationships. "Bernstein had no great love affair during those student days," biographer Humphrey Burton wrote. "The love of his life was music." Also, Bernstein showed affection for both men and women, and he enjoyed intimate relationships with both sexes.

Bernstein, age 25

❦ SEVEN ❦

The Big Splash

By the summer of 1940, World War II and the Nazi reign of terror were ravaging Europe. After Hitler came to power in Germany, anti-Semitism became an official government policy. The German government stripped Jews of their citizenship, seized their property, and sent millions of them to concentration camps. As anti-Semitism spread, the world grew more fearful. Jews in America, for example, were often urged to change their names to protect their jobs. Even Serge Koussevitzky suggested that Lenny change his name to Lenny S. Burns (the "S" for Samuel). Koussevitzky wanted to remove any roadblocks to Lenny's success in the music world, and he thought that the new name would be "more presentable" for a conductor. Lenny rejected the idea though. He was too proud of his name and his heritage to disguise them.

Koussevitzky eventually became Lenny's surrogate father, and Tanglewood became the young man's spiritual and musical home. He hated to leave at the end of the summer—especially to return to the cold environment of the Curtis Institute.

Lenny's last year at Curtis, however, was far different from the first. He was the only conducting student, up to that time, who had received an A from Fritz Reiner. By 1941 he had captured the attention and admiration of three of the world's greatest conductors—Dimitri Mitropoulos, Fritz Reiner, and Serge Koussevitzky. Although all three had a lasting impact on Lenny, it was Mitropoulos's unique style of conducting without a baton that the young maestro adopted at first. He explained that the movements he made with his hands were similar to those made while playing the piano. The index finger acted just like a baton. Once

Bernstein often emulated Dimitri Mitropoulos's style by conducting with his hands instead of using a baton.

convinced, Lenny's instructors allowed him to conduct in his own style.

During his last year at Curtis, Lenny continued to see his good friends, including composers Paul Bowles, whom he had met in New York, and David Diamond and Shirley Gabis, whom he met in Philadelphia while at Curtis. He continued to write to Helen Coates, whose advice ("eat sensibly and regularly") was not always taken but whose praise ("bravo— a thousand times") was encouraging. Her "bravo" referred to Lenny's final performance at Curtis in 1941. For that special occasion he conducted the Curtis Institute orchestra in Johannes Brahms's A Major Serenade. He was also in a concert given by Madame Vengerova's piano pupils. He received an A$^+$ in piano and As in the rest of his courses. At last, on May 3, 1941, he received his diploma. Aaron Copland came to his graduation, which to Lenny was an added honor.

Lenny wondered if he would ever get a chance to conduct a major symphony orchestra. "Stop complaining," Copland told him. "You are destined for success." But Lenny was never sure. At the same time, Sam Bernstein kept asking, "Where's the money?"

Lenny couldn't wait to return to Tanglewood for the summer. Once there, he relaxed and basked in the joy of being called Koussevitzky's protégé, but the concern about finding a steady job continued to haunt him. With the United States on the brink of entering World War II, he also thought about being drafted. Because of his chronic asthma, however, he was classified 4F, disqualified for medical reasons. "It was humiliating and frustrating for Lenny not to be in uniform while just about everyone else was preparing for war, but there was nothing to be done."

Between the Tanglewood seasons of 1941 and 1942,

Lenny rented a small studio in Boston in hopes of teaching piano, but in the shadow of war, students were scarce. He moved to New York in September 1942. Lenny worked on the *Lamentations*—a composition for soprano and orchestra—which evolved into his *Jeremiah,* Symphony No. 1. He entered the work in a competition but failed to win an award. Still, he was happy that its Jewish themes thrilled his father, to whom the work was dedicated.

The 1943 summer sessions at Tanglewood were canceled because of the war, but Koussevitzky, who lived near Tanglewood, wanted to help the war effort by giving a benefit concert for the Red Cross. He asked Lenny to assist him. When Lenny arrived at Serenak, Koussevitzky's estate, the maestro had a surprise for him—a message from Artur Rodzinski, the new music director of the New York Philharmonic Orchestra. Rodzinski lived close by and wanted to meet Lenny.

On August 25, 1943, Bernstein's twenty-fifth birthday, he and Artur Rodzinski met for the first time. Impressed by the way Lenny conducted the student orchestra at Tanglewood, Rodzinski invited Lenny to be his assistant conductor in New York. It was a birthday present Lenny Bernstein would never forget.

Lenny knew that the chances of an assistant conductor actually conducting the New York Philharmonic Orchestra before an audience in Carnegie Hall were next to none. "Established conductors had a notorious reputation for reaching the podium [even] with the aid of crutches," Burton Bernstein noted. Still, the thrill of rehearsing with one of the world's greatest orchestras satisfied Lenny. And Sam and Jennie were thrilled that their son had a job with a decent salary. Even so, Sam kept a job open for him at home. Lenny moved into

New York Philharmonic conductor Artur Rodzinski, right, *took on Bernstein,* left, *as his assistant conductor in 1943.*

an apartment in the Carnegie Hall building, where he worked.

Adding to the excitement, invitations to perform *Jeremiah* came from both Fritz Reiner and Serge Koussevitzky. First, however, Lenny had a special performance to attend. He had written a cycle of children's songs called *I Hate Music.* His friend Jennie Tourel would be singing the song cycle in her debut recital at New York's Town Hall on November 13, 1943.

Lenny insisted that his family come to New York for the

Carnegie Hall, home of the New York Philharmonic, pictured here in the early 1940s

recital. Sam, Jennie, and eleven-year-old Burton boarded a train for New York. Shirley was attending Mount Holyoke College at the time and couldn't come.

On the morning of the recital, Lenny received a phone call from Bruno Zirato, the Philharmonic's associate manager, informing him that Bruno Walter, who was to be the guest conductor of the New York Philharmonic the next day, was ill. Rodzinski was stranded by a snowstorm at his home near Tanglewood. If Walter's health did not improve by the following morning, Lenny would have to be ready to substitute for him. The opportunity seemed too bizarre to believe, and Lenny continued to focus on the Tourel recital.

When *I Hate Music* was well received, Lenny felt happy and relieved. He and Jennie celebrated the event at a post-recital party, where everyone laughed, sang, and drank until dawn. He could usually sleep late the day after such a bash—but not after that party.

At nine o'clock the next morning, November 14, 1943, Lenny was awakened by a phone call from Zirato. He told Lenny that Bruno Walter was still too sick to conduct the New York Philharmonic that afternoon. Lenny would have to fill in—with no time for rehearsal. He called his parents and told them not to leave New York. Instead, he told them to go to Carnegie Hall where tickets for the afternoon concert would be waiting for them.

When they heard the news, Sam and Jennie were stunned. "*Oy, gevalt!*" Burton remembered his astonished parents saying at the same time, "both of them holding their cheeks, as if to prevent their faces from collapsing."

As Carnegie Hall filled up and the lights dimmed, Lenny—"looking much younger and less elegant than the orchestra musicians," Burton Bernstein noted—"sort of

Bernstein's captivating stage presence and unique conducting style charmed critics and listeners alike.

hopped onto the podium." When the concert ended, the audience "roared like one giant animal in a zoo," Burton said. The fact that the concert had been broadcast on radio made it even more significant. Lenny was well known in circles around Boston, Tanglewood, and New York, but he was a total stranger to audiences around the United States—until that day.

Music lovers throughout the country heard the concert via CBS radio. In those war-torn days, radio bound the nation together in a way that no other medium could. Because of that, Bernstein's debut broadcast became "a national event." For the first time, the entire radio audience heard a major symphony orchestra conducted by an American-born and American-trained conductor.

Not surprisingly, well-known music critic Virgil Thomson was shocked by Bernstein's untraditional style. Conducting without a baton was the least of Thomson's complaints. "[Bernstein] shagged, he shimmied, and believe it or not, he *bumped,*" Thomson reported. But it was that very style that awakened the audience and inspired the musicians.

Even Sam began to think that selling beauty supplies might not be Lenny's calling after all. Musician and author William Westbrook Burton summed up the national reaction to the concert, saying that Bernstein "carried off what was probably the most sensational debut of any American conductor in this century." The concert even made the front page of the *New York Times.* The article said, "Mr. Bernstein had to have something approaching genius to make full use of his opportunity."

"That concert, of course, changed my life," Bernstein said.

Bernstein conducting the New York City Symphony, 1945

❧ EIGHT ❧

Hits and Misses

*For the present we "abstract" artists, we musicians
and dancers, have this to say to ourselves: Relax.
Invent. Perform. Have fun.*

—Leonard Bernstein

The spotlight that focused on Bernstein after his debut
seemed to leave music director Artur Rodzinski in the
shadows. The older conductor was not comfortable playing
second fiddle to the dazzling young star, so after three months
as assistant conductor of the New York Philharmonic,
Bernstein resigned.

In 1944 he accepted Fritz Reiner's invitation to conduct
the *Jeremiah* Symphony in Pittsburgh. Paul Bowles praised
the world premiere performance in the *New York Herald
Tribune*. "This work," he wrote, "outranks every other
symphonic product by any American composer of what is
called the younger generation." Jeremiah is the name of the
prophet "who God held directly accountable," Bernstein

explained. "I wouldn't say that God is up there watching over me, as much as me down here looking up to find Him—I guess you would call that a chief concern of my life."

That same year, Bernstein collaborated with choreographer Jerome Robbins on his ballet *Fancy Free*—a smash hit about three sailors on a twenty-four-hour leave in New York City. It was later expanded into the Broadway musical *On the Town,* with book and lyrics by Adolph Green and Betty Comden. Bernstein's innovative mix of jazzy American folk styles and symphonic forms reflected the spirit of the 1940s and made history on Broadway.

Lenny's sister Shirley sang in the chorus of *On the Town.* By then she had graduated from college and moved into Lenny's New York apartment. She loved being a part of his upbeat life and enjoyed his illustrious friends. And Lenny loved having her there. As their younger brother, Burton, grew older, he, too, shared in the good times that sprang from Lenny's success. All three were determined to keep the world of Rybernia alive.

Unable to resist the vitality and joy of Broadway, Lenny managed to juggle both composing and conducting. It was difficult to shift gears as often as he did, especially when his beloved mentor Koussevitzky urged him to get back to conducting—for which he had trained so hard and earned so much praise. Koussevitzky hoped that Bernstein would succeed him as conductor of the Boston Symphony Orchestra someday.

As a stepping-stone to that post, Bernstein was offered the position of musical director of the New York City Symphony—known as the City Center Orchestra—on his twenty-seventh birthday. He succeeded the renowned Leopold Stokowski, who had become famous when he conducted the

Bernstein rehearses the New York City Symphony.

Philadelphia Orchestra in the Walt Disney animated film *Fantasia*. As conductor of the City Center Orchestra, Bernstein introduced contemporary American composers to his audiences while continuing to present the standard classical composers. Olin Downes of the *New York Times* said that Bernstein's first concert was marked by extraordinary vitality and showed "exceptional brilliance." A few weeks later, Bernstein conducted Tchaikovsky's *Concert Fantasy for Piano and Orchestra*, featuring the distinguished young American pianist Leo Smit. Olin Downes marveled at the orchestra's improvement in the few weeks since Bernstein became director.

The new conductor expressed concern for the welfare of his musicians. Bernstein worked to initiate pay raises, extend the season to twenty-four weeks so the musicians had more working hours, and secure a recording contract and radio sponsor. Bernstein also began a custom that allowed anyone in the orchestra to "consult him about anything, including . . . personal problems."

Bernstein had personal problems of his own at the time. Despite Koussevitzky's efforts on behalf of his protégé, the trustees of the Boston Symphony Orchestra rejected Bernstein as Koussevitzky's successor. Some Bostonians believed anti-Semitism played a part in the decision. Others thought that Bernstein's image as a "youth who played boogie-woogie, who danced on tables in restaurants, as [he] had been seen to do at Tanglewood, and had a hit musical on Broadway" irritated the staid Boston board of trustees.

Bernstein dealt with his disappointment by throwing himself into his work with the City Center Orchestra. Harold Schonberg, a *New York Times* music critic, wrote: "When he was with the City Center Orchestra, it was the most exciting, the most vital that I ever heard from him on the podium." The whole orchestra seemed to have fun under Bernstein's direction, and he lured his talented friends into performing with the financially strapped orchestra without a fee. He even persuaded the famous Chilean pianist Claudio Arrau to perform. One of Arrau's guests at his performance in February 1946 was a Chilean actress, Felicia Montealegre, who had been studying piano with him in New York. At a postconcert party at Arrau's house, Bernstein met Felicia, and a romance soon began. "She's an angel and a wonderful companion," Lenny wrote to Helen Coates. "She fits so well into any situation—on a horse or bicycle, at a party, or alone together."

Felicia Montealegre, pictured here in a production of Rudyard Kipling's The Light That Failed

Bernstein, center, *remained close with his sister Shirley,* left, *and brother Burton,* right, *for his entire life.*

That summer Felicia joined Lenny at Tanglewood for the first full session there since the end of the war in 1945. As usual, he was the center of attention—always surrounded by eager students and admiring colleagues and guests. Jean Shaw, a piano student at the time, talked about the magical summer of 1946 under Bernstein's spell. "We were all enchanted by him," she said. "He was the spark that ignited our enthusiasm and love of music . . . and he insisted that *everyone* call him Lenny!"

The highlight of the summer was the American premiere of Benjamin Britten's opera *Peter Grimes,* which Bernstein conducted at Koussevitzky's request. To fourteen-year-old Burton Bernstein, however, it was the reminder of Rybernia that made the summer so special. Both he and Shirley stayed at Lenny's lakeshore cottage along with many of Lenny's old friends, including Adolph Green and David Diamond, as well as Felicia. Helen Coates, who had become Lenny's beloved personal secretary and confidante, tried to keep order amidst the chaos in the crowded cottage. It reminded Burton of summers in Sharon. "I was captivated by all the delightful chaos and all those 'crazy artist nuts,' as Sam called them."

Lenny, Shirley, and Burton continued to meet at Tanglewood when Burton was on vacation from Dartmouth College and Shirley was between jobs in New York. Whenever possible, they would travel together during Lenny's concert tours. In 1948 Lenny and Burton drove to Taos, New Mexico, with the British poet Stephen Spender. They stayed at a secluded ranch where Spender could write and Lenny could work on *The Age of Anxiety,* his second symphony, based on a poem by W. H. Auden.

When *The Age of Anxiety,* dedicated to Koussevitzky, was first performed on April 8, 1949, it received mixed reviews. As

Bernstein plays with the Israel Philharmonic Orchestra at Beersheba in 1948 during Israel's War of Independence.

critic David Denby wrote, "The best thing in the Second Symphony . . . is the fifth movement, 'Masque,' in which the piano and the xylophone, lithe and happy together, produce the scintillating effect of needles flashing through the air." But he thought the work ended badly.

In the late 1940s and early 1950s, Bernstein continued to compose and conduct, taking a few months off to write music for the American theater. In 1948, during Israel's War of Independence, he played piano and conducted the Israel Philharmonic Orchestra in a desert in Israel, where the musicians sat in chairs perched on rocks. The orchestra played the moving *Resurrection* symphony by Gustav Mahler while Israeli prime minister David Ben-Gurion and five thousand Israeli troops listened in awe. Performing the concert in the midst of a war was risky but highly rewarding—especially for Bernstein, who had strong feelings about Israel's struggle to establish and hold on to its homeland, then under attack by the surrounding Arab nations.

Bernstein decided to spend 1951 in Mexico for a period of rest and concentration. One day he received a phone call from Olga Koussevitzky. She gave him the sad news that her husband was gravely ill. Lenny rushed back to Boston to be with his "musical father." "In two hours I am on a plane; that night I am at his bedside . . . . The next day he is gone." Bernstein never forgot the important role Koussevitzky played in his career or "the festive spirit that surrounded his concerts" and the depth of Koussevitzky's feeling for music.

Three months later, on September 9, 1951, Lenny and Felicia were married at Temple Mishkan Tefila. The reception was held at the Bernstein home in Brookline—a Boston suburb where the family had moved in 1944. Sam and Jennie

Bernstein were particularly pleased that Felicia, who was half-Jewish, agreed to a Jewish wedding. During the course of their marriage, Felicia and Lenny had three children. Jamie was born in 1952, Alexander Serge (named after Serge Koussevitzky) in 1955, and Nina in 1962.

Bernstein's one-act opera, *Trouble in Tahiti,* was performed on June 12, 1952, at the Brandeis Festival in Waltham, Massachusetts, and received mixed reviews. Some reviewers claimed the music was lively, but the subject (a deteriorating marriage) was "dreary." Humphrey Burton called the work an important breakthrough in musical

Bernstein married Felicia Montealegre in 1951.

Bernstein with Felicia, left, *Alexander,* center, *and Jamie,* right, *in 1956*

theater, however. "Bernstein was pushing forward into emotional territory that nobody in American musical theater had previously dared to explore," he wrote. *"Tahiti* was a key work in his [Bernstein's] development."

In 1953 family and friends gathered in New York for Bernstein's Broadway hit, *Wonderful Town.* Harold Schonberg, often a harsh critic, wrote, *"Wonderful Town* is sophisticated and full of musical ideas, full of musical wit, too." Deems Taylor, another respected critic, "thought Bernstein was a wonderful talent . . . without doubt a young man of genius."

In the late 1950s, Bernstein began a nationally broadcast series of *Young People's Concerts*, using television as a medium for teaching children about music.

❧ NINE ❧

Communication – Bernstein Style

Let us say that love is the way we have of communicating personally in the deepest way. Music can . . . extend this communication, magnify it, and carry it to vastly greater numbers of people.

—Leonard Bernstein

In 1954 Bernstein found the ideal way to fulfill his need to share and to connect with others through the CBS television series *Omnibus*. Through that series, Bernstein hoped to "clear away the usual pomposity and condescension of 'music appreciation.'" The programs captivated viewers.

For the first show, artists had painted the entire floor of the set with every note of the opening page of Beethoven's Fifth Symphony. Bernstein walked in and out of the musical notes on the floor as the musicians played the notes there. He showed how the entire first movement of the symphony is

Bernstein wrote the music for the 1954 film On the Waterfront, *an unflinching account of corrupt New York City harbor unions. The film starred Marlon Brando,* right, *and Rod Steiger,* left.

based on the first four notes. The show's entertaining yet educational format attracted both children and adults. Bernstein continued this style of teaching in his Young People's Concerts, which were first televised in January 1958 on CBS television. Bernstein charmed his viewers:

> He was full of mischief: he ravished the children with flattery, playing excerpts of difficult works [on the piano] by Webern and Stravinsky, and then, in the next moment, drawing on examples from pop—Elvis, the Beatles, Simon and Garfunkel—all of which he obviously loved.

Bernstein also discussed the elements of music—including melody, harmony, and rhythm. He used examples ranging from songs by the popular American composer George Gershwin to operas by the classical German composer Richard Wagner. Bernstein "may have done more to create music lovers than anyone but the great composers themselves." The television programs inspired Bernstein's book *The Joy of Music,* first published in 1959.

But television shows were only a part of Bernstein's busy schedule. He managed to finish his satirical opera *Candide,* which he had begun in 1951, working with playwright Lillian Hellman. The opera was based on a fable about injustice written by the French philosopher Voltaire in 1759. *Candide* opened in New York on December 1, 1956, but ran for fewer than eighty performances.

Bernstein kept his audience enraptured by incorporating modern pop music into his Young People's Concerts.

Bernstein, standing center, *leads a rehearsal for* West Side Story.

The following year, 1957, Bernstein worked with songwriter Stephen Sondheim, choreographer Jerome Robbins, and playwright Arthur Laurents, on the musical *West Side Story. West Side Story,* a modern interpretation of William Shakespeare's *Romeo and Juliet,* broke all records on Broadway and on stages throughout the world. The music's changing rhythms reflected the explosive atmosphere of New York tenement life, ethnic gangs, violence, and intense love and hate. To emphasize the contrasting cultures and emotions, Bernstein paired classical music with the Latin

dance forms of Jerome Robbins. Both the story and the
music showed remarkable foresight and beauty.

> When the beautiful "Tonight" is reprised, with another
> solo voice and with the two gangs (in a different
> rhythm) joining the lovers, the cross-rhythms coa-
> lesce, and suddenly Bernstein is where he wants to
> be—soaring with Mozart and Verdi in a five-part en-
> semble. It's a thrilling moment.

While he was enjoying his success on Broadway,
Bernstein was also codirecting the New York Philharmonic

Choreographer Jerome Robbins, center, *worked on both the stage
production of* West Side Story *and the film version,* above.

Bernstein conducts a working rehearsal of the New York Philharmonic.

Orchestra with Dimitri Mitropoulos. In 1958, after Mitropoulos's departure, Bernstein became the music director, putting him at the pinnacle of both the concert hall and musical theater. "It was a double-act that few could follow." Bernstein had been a great Broadway idol, and he made the transition from Broadway to the concert platform—a feat no one else had ever accomplished.

During Lenny's seven-week tour of Latin America with the New York Philharmonic, he and Felicia visited Chile, Felicia's homeland. At a concert in Santiago, Bernstein opened with a brisk rendition of Chile's national anthem. Felicia was thrilled. She said, "I had never imagined I'd hear my husband conduct the national anthem there, where I grew up. It was a beautiful extraordinary moment and the tears were streaming from my face. It meant coming home in glory."

As director of the Philharmonic, Bernstein had little time to compose. He did manage to finish his *Kaddish,* the Third Symphony (based on a Jewish prayer), in which he expressed his feelings toward his father. He also completed the *Chichester Psalms,* but his chief focus was on the orchestra. He was building up the orchestra's financial base, adding money for recordings and television presentations, and enhancing the Philharmonic's global reputation with tours to Europe, Russia, and South America. Under Bernstein's leadership, the musicians became full-time employees under contract.

Yet the urge to focus on composing grew stronger, and in 1969 he decided to leave his post as musical director. On his departure he was given the prestigious title of Conductor Laureate—an honor he treasured.

Bernstein is flanked by his proud and loving parents.

❦ TEN ❦

Triumphs and Tragedies

The 1960s brought personal tragedy to Lenny. Sam Bernstein suffered a heart attack in 1964 and was in and out of the hospital from then until his death at Boston's Beth Israel Hospital on April 30, 1969, the year Lenny retired from the Philharmonic. At his seventieth birthday celebration on January 7, 1962, Sam had received high praise from his children. Honoring his father, Lenny said, "I think that probably the greatest gift my father bestowed on us children was to teach us to love learning." Sam enjoyed the celebration, and, according to Burton Bernstein, he especially enjoyed a piece Lenny prepared for his father that was based on a klezmer tune Sam used to sing in the shower.

The 1960s marked the assassinations of President John F. Kennedy (1963), civil rights leader Martin Luther King Jr. (1968), and Senator Robert F. Kennedy (1968). At the same time, war escalated in Vietnam.

In honor of the late president, who, with his wife, Jacqueline, had actively promoted the arts in the United States, the John F. Kennedy Center for the Performing Arts was built in

93

Bernstein, first row, center, *and cast members of Bernstein's* Mass, *composed in honor of President John F. Kennedy, take their bows after the Kennedy Center's inaugural performance in 1971.*

Washington, D.C. The president's widow, Jacqueline Kennedy Onassis, asked Bernstein to compose a special work for the center's opening in 1971.

Bernstein's *Mass,* an antiwar composition dedicated to John F. Kennedy, drew mixed reviews. "It's stupendous. Jack would have loved it," the president's mother, Rose Kennedy, said. Critic John Simon called it "rather vulgar." Paul Hume said, "it was the greatest music Bernstein had ever written." Harold Schonberg labeled it "pretentious and thin."

As usual, without missing a beat, Bernstein moved on to other ventures. In 1973 he delivered six Charles Eliot Norton Lectures at Harvard. His lectures spawned his book *The Unanswered Question* just as his television shows had inspired *The Joy of Music.* His books express his love of music and music as communication.

Bernstein left for Rome during the summer of 1973 to conduct the Italian Radio Orchestra in a concert for Pope Paul VI at the Vatican. Bernstein brought his family—Felicia, Jamie, Alex, and Nina—and Helen Coates and Julia Vega, their Chilean housekeeper, for the special event. The concert was an extraordinary experience for them all, especially for Felicia, who had been raised as a Catholic.

Although Lenny's marriage to Felicia appeared ideal, it was not. Lenny had sexual relationships with members of both sexes. As a bisexual person, he had had various relationships with other men, but the one with musicologist Tom Cothran had the most serious consequences. Felicia and Lenny separated in 1976. Lenny had become intimately involved with Tom, who urged Bernstein to move in with him. Lenny loved

Although his marriage and family life were important to him, Bernstein chose to separate from his wife, Felicia, in 1976 to be with longtime companion Tom Cothran.

his wife and his three children, and they missed the family life they had shared at home in New York City and in Fairfield, Connecticut. "He was fun to have around," his daughter Jamie wrote in a *Newsweek* magazine article. "There were always musicians in the house . . . loud, raucous, funny people . . . singing at the piano."

Bernstein, too, began to miss his family life. He missed the close bond he had had with Felicia and the children. Finally, in 1977, he left Tom Cothran and reconciled with Felicia. On June 15, the *New York Daily News* reported, "the Leonard Bernsteins are together and everyone is hoping it will stick." Family life once again resumed, and Lenny's travel whirlwind continued.

The entire family attended a Leonard Bernstein Festival in Israel that same year. Jamie noted in her diary that her father, looking "ancient, hallowed," resembled the Jehovah figure while conducting his *Kaddish* symphony in Israel. Next, Bernstein went to Paris where he gave a concert for cancer research. With typical nonstop energy, he went on to Vienna to perform with the Vienna Philharmonic.

Felicia had been diagnosed with lung cancer, probably a result of heavy smoking. She moved into a house in East Hampton, Long Island, to be near the Bernsteins' good friends Phyllis and Adolph Green and to have a view of the sea. Felicia underwent chemotherapy sessions in the fall of 1977 and heart surgery that November. Despite her condition, she joined Lenny in Vienna in January 1978. Her hair had fallen out as a result of the chemotherapy, so she wore an elegant hat over her bald head. On February 5, Lenny gave a festive party in Vienna to celebrate her fifty-sixth birthday and the thirty-second anniversary of their meeting.

"The Viennese musicians appeared to have a love affair

with Bernstein." One orchestra member said, "Bernstein opened all doors with us because he had the courage to translate all his feelings into movements without restraint." He had the courage to show his emotions ranging from joy to sadness—through his physical movements and facial expressions while conducting.

Bernstein's chief goal in Vienna was to restore the music of the great Jewish composer Gustav Mahler—music that Hitler had banned. "His music is so close to my heart," Bernstein said, "—the nostalgia for childhood, the innocent times—I love even his weaknesses, and perhaps some of them are my own." His daughter Jamie explained, "My father had his musical peak experiences with them [the Vienna Philharmonic Orchestra], *no question.*"

Schuyler Chapin, head of Columbia Records Masterworks

Bernstein leads the Vienna Philharmonic in Gustav Mahler's Ninth Symphony.

Division at the time, believed that Bernstein's recordings of Mahler's music reveal the "best and fullest moments of artistic expression." Chapin helped Bernstein form Amberson Productions—organized to develop recordings, films, and other media ventures—a part of Amberson Enterprises, which oversaw Lenny's business affairs. "Next to my own wife and children," Chapin wrote, "I think Leonard Bernstein was the most liberating influence on my life. He taught me never to be afraid of passion and never to stop exploring the world. He was the older brother I never had, the teacher I'd always missed."

Bernstein cut short his European trip when he heard that

Bernstein and his wife, Felicia

Felicia was close to death. Felicia tried to remain hopeful about beating her cancer, but she could not do so for long. She died on June 16, 1978. Although cancer had been diagnosed as the cause of her death, Lenny blamed himself. He believed that the turmoil and depression he had caused her led to her death. "His sense of guilt never left him." Only through music could he relieve his own depression caused by her loss.

Bernstein continued conducting throughout the 1980s. Although he was in great demand around the world, Bernstein also returned to composing. In 1983 his opera *A Quiet Place,* a story of the suffering and loss of a loved one, was performed at the Houston Grand Opera. In that opera, Bernstein tackles deep personal issues, including those of a father who finally accepts his gay son. The *Village Voice* newspaper called *A Quiet Place* "the birth of a powerful new opera." The work seemed to fulfill Bernstein's hope of composing "one real moving American opera that any American can understand."

In 1986 Bernstein conducted a special concert of his own music for Queen Elizabeth and Prince Philip in London. Later, he opened the Schleswig-Holstein Festival—styled after Tanglewood—in Kiel, Germany. While there he introduced his first European teaching course for young conductors.

Bernstein remarked, "I don't feel vindicated as a composer, but I do as a teacher." His students knew why. Recalling her summers at Tanglewood, Jean Shaw concluded: "There were many teachers who could expand your knowledge of music...but with Lenny—you fell in love with it."

Although Bernstein was suffering from emphysema and lung cancer, he continued to conduct as much as possible and wherever possible. He even conducted at the Berlin Wall

Germans celebrate the fall of the Berlin Wall, above. *Bernstein gave a concert in Berlin to celebrate this historic event.*

in Germany. The Berlin Wall, built in 1961, had been one of the most visible symbols of division—as well as a physical barrier—between the Communism of the Soviet Union and the Democracy of the Free World. In the fall of 1989, as Communism was collapsing in Eastern Europe, the Berlin Wall that had divided East Berlin and West Berlin was dismantled. To celebrate the country's reunification, Bernstein gave a concert on Christmas Day. His orchestra included musicians from both sides of the divided city. The historic orchestra played Beethoven's Ninth Symphony as hundreds of local citizens joined visitors from around the world to listen and cheer. Bernstein changed Beethoven's words "Ode to Joy" to "Ode to Freedom," and the concert became known worldwide as the Freedom Concert.

That concert "was the highest point in Leonard Bernstein's public life as a citizen of the world," David Denby wrote in the *New Yorker*. "He believed in the universal language of art and believed music to be the art best equipped to dissolve borders and reconcile differences—it was as if Beethoven's Ninth with its message of universal brotherhood was constantly playing in his head."

Despite failing health, Bernstein continued to conduct well into his later years.

❦ ELEVEN ❦

"A Summer Dream Called Tanglewood"

Follow, poet, follow right
To the bottom of the night,
With your unconstraining voice
Still persuade us to rejoice.

—W. H. Auden

Bernstein continued his concert tours despite the coughing, wheezing, and breathlessness caused by his lung cancer and emphysema. In 1990 he inaugurated the Pacific Music Festival (a Japanese version of Tanglewood) in Sapporo, Japan. In a wavering voice, he delivered his dedication speech:

> [I want] to devote most of the remaining energy and time the Lord grants me to education, sharing as much as I can with younger people—especially very much younger people—whatever I know not only

> about music but also art, and not only about the arts,
> but also about the relation between art and life. And
> about being oneself, finding one's self, "knowing who
> you are," and doing the best possible job. If I can com-
> municate some of this . . . I will be a happy man.

When he collapsed during his stay in Tokyo, however, Bernstein left Japan and returned to New York. Worried family members were there to greet him, but nothing they said could stop him from conducting a special memorial concert in honor of Serge Koussevitzky at Tanglewood. With the help of painkillers and other medications, he was ready for the concert on August 19, 1990.

On that day, Bernstein's family and friends joined throngs of others who drove up to the "green mountain of youth and joy in the glorious summer dream we called Tanglewood," as Bernstein described it. They came to witness Bernstein and the Boston Symphony Orchestra celebrate the fiftieth anniversary of the famous music school and honor the memory of its founder, Serge Koussevitzky. But could the ailing Bernstein even walk to the podium—let alone conduct Beethoven's Seventh Symphony? "Knowing Bernstein, he'll pull it off—somehow," a hopeful student said. And he did. It was the performance of a lifetime:

> He nearly broke down in the middle of the Beethoven
> . . . gasping for breath. Yet he kept on, clearly deter-
> mined to make this the performance of a lifetime,
> bringing out an extraordinary amount of detail from
> the score while never losing track of its central pulse.
> Rarely have the symphony's silences seemed so
> portentous, its climaxes so exultant.

Bernstein canceled the rest of his concert schedule and returned to his New York apartment. He officially announced his retirement, which sent shock waves through the music world—just as his debut had done forty-seven years earlier. People had come to think of Leonard Bernstein as indestructible. He would never retire, they thought. But he did. He had to.

Bernstein remained in his apartment, where family, friends, longtime personal physician Dr. Kevin Cahill, and others brought him comfort and cheer. Bernstein's condition worsened, however, and on Sunday afternoon, October 14, 1990, he suffered a heart attack and died.

Two days later, after a family service in New York, Bernstein was buried next to his wife in the Green Wood Cemetery in Brooklyn. As the funeral motorcade proceeded slowly from 72nd Street to the Brooklyn side of the East River, construction workers along the route removed their hard hats and waved. "Good-bye, Lenny!" they called out. "I can't think of anything—*anything*—that would have pleased Lenny more than that," his brother Burton said.

In his eulogy, Burton Bernstein went right to the heart of his brother's life:

> He wanted the whole world to love itself into one big happy family, and he took it as a personal affront when the world refused to comply. He maintained unflinching optimism and religious trust in the ultimate improvability of man, despite all the hard evidence to the contrary. Lenny was in love with love.

Epilogue

Burton Bernstein, brother of Leonard Bernstein, has given permission for the use of the following excerpt from the eulogy he delivered at his brother's memorial service in New York on October 16, 1990.

My brother, Lenny, who was always larger than life, turned out to be smaller than death. Amazingly—just like that!—he is no more. It seems impossible.

Those of us who were closest to him, who knew him best and longest, who loved him most, we—such lucky ones we are!—we somehow assumed that he would go on forever, like time itself, that he was somehow immortal, not just perishable matter like the rest of us.

There would, we felt, always be our Lenny doing what he did so passionately, so brilliantly, so charmingly, so originally, so lovingly, and, yes, sometimes so excessively—always so full of life and so much larger than life.

All the world knows what he did:

Teaching people—his favorite occupation, really. Descended from rabbis, he was a rabbi at heart, a master teacher. Just listening to Lenny was an education. (I know

107

this better than most because I was taught by Lenny from just about my first day on this earth.) There was nothing he'd rather do than stimulate new thoughts for, especially, young minds.

Making history. He *was* the living precedent for American music—the first American to be taken seriously on the concert stage. I think it can be said that he made it possible for any talented American kid to follow in his footsteps.

Experimenting with the new, even though he was a hopeless traditionalist. He welcomed the avant-garde but he cherished the pristine, lovely tune—the simple song.

Revivifying the old—which I believe was his greatest gift as a conductor. How often have we heard, as if for the first time, an *echt* [genuine] Lenny rendition of, say, Tchaikovsky's 5th or Brahms's 1st, and marveled at all the nuances we had missed over the years? How often have we seen and listened to him draw, through sheer love and musicianly example, unforgettable performances from orchestras—performances the musicians would later admit that they never knew they had in them? His very last concert—conducting Beethoven's 7th at Tanglewood—was only the most recent case in point.

Preaching love and peace. Naively, he wanted the whole world to love itself into one big happy family, and he took it as a personal affront when the world refused to comply. He maintained unflinching optimism and religious trust in the ultimate improvability of man, despite all the hard evidence to the contrary. Lenny was in love with love.

Helping young talent and his less-celebrated, less-lucky contemporaries, some of whom responded to his kindness with rank envy and disloyalty, which, typically, Lenny was quick to ignore and forgive . . . .

All those things that were Lenny are no more . . . and that

108

terrible fact is unbelievable and unbearable. And yet, of course, the great, obvious cliché that springs to mind is quite true: Lenny is immortal, after all. The memories of him will be there, along with the recordings and the revivals and the writings, for generations upon generations. Just as long as people care a damn about something finer in life than power and money and their imagined superiority over others there will always be Lenny around to educate, entertain, edify, move, and inspire—to change us all in some wonderful, subtle way.

In that sense, Lenny is larger than mere death, too.

—Burton Bernstein
October 16, 1990

Bernstein with his wife and three children

Timeline

1918 Born in Lawrence, Massachusetts, on August 25

1923 Sister, Shirley Anne, born on October 23

1928 First piano lessons, with Frieda Karp

1932 Brother, Burton, born on January 31; begins
      piano lessons with Helen Coates

1934 Adapts, produces, and plays title role in *Carmen*

1935 Enters Harvard University and studies piano with
      Heinrich Gebhard

1937 Meets Dimitri Mitropoulos and Aaron Copland

1939 Directs Harvard performance of Blitzstein's
      The Cradle Will Rock; graduates Harvard, *cum laude,*
      and enrolls as a conducting student of Fritz Reiner
      at the Curtis Institute

1940 Student of Serge Koussevitzky at Tanglewood; conducts
      Boston Pops

1941 Receives diploma in conducting from Curtis Institute

1942 Completes first symphony, *Jeremiah*

1943 Premiere of *I Hate Music*, by Jennie Tourel and Leonard
      Bernstein, in Lenox, Massachussets; becomes assistant
      conductor of the New York Philharmonic Orchestra;
      first solo recording as a pianist, playing David
      Diamond's Prelude and Fugue No. 3 in C# Major;
      premiere of *I Hate Music* by Jennie Tourel in Town Hall,
      New York City; makes debut as conductor of the New York
      Philharmonic when guest conductor Bruno Walter
      becomes ill

1944   First performance of the ballet *Fancy Free*, for
       which Bernstein wrote the music; *On the Town*
       premieres in New York City

1945   Becomes director of the New York City Symphony—
       known as the City Center Orchestra

1946   Overseas debut with Czech Philharmonic, Prague

1948   Musical adviser to Israel Philharmonic Orchestra;
       conducts concert at Beersheba, Israel, during Israel's
       War of Independence

1949   Premiere of *The Age of Anxiety,* Symphony No. 2.;
       MGM film of *On the Town* opens

1951   Bernstein and Koussevitzky start three-month
       tour coconducting the Israel Philharmonic Orchestra;
       marries Felicia Montealegre

1952   Daughter, Jamie Anne Maria, is born on September 8

1953   Premiere of *Wonderful Town* in New York City

1954   Columbia Pictures film *On the Waterfront* opens; first
       Omnibus telecast airs

1955   Son, Alexander Serge Leonard, is born on July 7

1956   Signs first long-term music contract with Columbia
       Records (later CBS); named principal conductor
       (with Dimitri Mitropoulos) of the New York Philharmonic
       Orchestra; premiere of *Candide* in New York City

1957   Conducts the inaugural concert at Frederic R. Mann
       Auditorium in Tel Aviv, Israel; premiere of *West Side
       Story* in New York City

1958   Directs first concert as coconductor of the New York
       Philharmonic Orchestra; first New York Philharmonic
       Orchestra's Young People's Concert airs; begins appointment
       as co-music-director of the New York Philharmonic Orchestra

1959   *The Joy of Music* is published

1961   United Artists film of *West Side Story* opens

1962   Daughter, Nina Maria Felicia, is born on February 28

1963   Leads the New York Philharmonic Orchestra in the
        John F. Kennedy memorial concert on CBS-TV; first
        performance of third symphony, *Kaddish,* in Tel Aviv,
        Israel

1966   First engagements with London Symphony Orchestra
        and the Vienna Philharmonic Orchestra; *The Infinite
        Variety of Music* is published

1967   Conducts the Israel Philharmonic Orchestra on Mount
        Scopus in Jerusalem after the Six-Day War

1969   Father, Samuel J. Bernstein, dies on April 30; retires
        from the New York Philharmonic Orchestra and is
        named Conductor Laureate of the orchestra

1971   Inaugurates the John F. Kennedy Center for the
        Performing Arts, Washington, D.C., with the premiere
        performance of *Mass*

1973   Delivers Charles Eliot Norton Lectures at Harvard;
        leads concerts at the Vatican, Rome, to celebrate
        the tenth anniversary of Paul VI's papacy

1976   *The Unanswered Question* is published; separates
        from Felicia to live with Tom Cothran

1977   Reconciles with Felicia

1978   Felicia Montealegre Bernstein dies on June 16

1982   *Findings* is published

1983   Premiere of *A Quiet Place*

1984   Daughter Jamie marries David Evan Thomas

1985   Journey for Peace event at Hiroshima, Japan

1987   Granddaughter, Francisca Ann Maria Thomas, is born
on March 4

1988   Tours with the Vienna Philharmonic and London Symphony
Orchestras

1989   Grandson, Evan Samuel Thomas, is born on October 14;
conducts two Berlin Freedom Concerts to celebrate the
fall of the Berlin Wall in Germany

1990   Inaugurates the Pacific Music Festival, Sapporo, Japan;
memorial concert for Koussevitzky at Tanglewood,
Bernstein's final performance; Leonard Bernstein dies
on October 14; memorial service in New York on October 16

Sources

p. 11 Burton Bernstein, *Family Matters: Sam, Jennie, and the Kids* (New York: Summit Books, 1982), 146–147.

p. 11 *Reaching for the Note*, directed by Susan Lacy, 117 min., Public Broadcasting System, 1998, digital video disk.

p. 11 Ibid.

p. 13 B. Bernstein, *Family Matters*, 22.

p. 14 Ibid., 41.

p. 20 Humphrey Burton, *Leonard Bernstein* (New York: Doubleday, 1994), 7.

p. 21 Ibid.; Ibid., 8.

p. 22 Ibid., 9.

pp. 22–23 B. Bernstein, *Family Matters*, 62.

p. 25 H. Burton, *Leonard Bernstein*, 10.

p. 26 Ibid., 11.

p. 26 B. Bernstein, *Family Matters*, 74.

p. 28 Ibid., 113; Ibid., 11.

p. 29 Leonard Bernstein, *Findings* (New York: Simon & Schuster, 1982), 14.

p. 29 B. Bernstein, *Family Matters*, 113.

p. 30 Ibid.

p. 31 H. Burton, *Leonard Bernstein*, 20.

p. 33 Ibid., 25.

p. 36 Meryle Secrest, *Leonard Bernstein: A Life* (New York: Alfred A. Knopf, 1994), 33.

p. 36 Ibid.

pp. 36–37 Ibid.

p. 37 B. Bernstein, *Family Matters*, 127.

p. 37 Ibid.

p. 37 H. Burton, *Leonard Bernstein*, 31.

p. 38 Ibid.

pp. 39–40 Ibid., 23.

p. 40 Ibid., 22.

p. 40 B. Bernstein, *Family Matters*, 129.

p. 40 Ibid.

p. 41 Ibid., 126.

p. 44 H. Burton, *Leonard Bernstein*, 34.

p. 44 Ibid., 35.

p. 44 Secrest, 39.

p. 44 Arthur Gelb et al., eds., *Great Lives of the Twentieth Century* (New York: The New York Times Company, 1988), 498.

p. 45 L. Bernstein, *Findings*, 270.

p. 45 Secrest, 39.

pp. 46–47 Ibid., 42.

p. 47 L. Bernstein, *Findings*, 286.

p. 48 Peter Evensen, interviewed by the author, 25 May 1999.

p. 48 H. Burton, *Leonard Bernstein*, 47.

p. 49 L. Bernstein, *Findings*, 287.

p. 49 Ibid., 288.

p. 50 H. Burton, *Leonard Bernstein*, 44.

p. 50 L. Bernstein, *Findings*, 321.

p. 53 Secrest, 54.

p. 54 H. Burton, *Leonard Bernstein*, 53.

p. 54 Ibid.

pp. 54–55 L. Bernstein, *Findings*, 227.

p. 56 Ibid., 320.

p. 57 Secrest, 66.

p. 57 Ibid.

pp. 57–58 Ibid.

pp. 58–59 B. Bernstein, *Family Matters,* 136–137.

p. 59 Secrest, 78.

p. 59 H. Burton, *Leonard Bernstein,* 76.

p. 60 Secrest, 80–81.

p. 61 H. Burton, *Leonard Bernstein,* 83.

p. 65 Ibid., 88.

p. 65 L. Bernstein, *Findings,* 290.

p. 65 H. Burton, *Leonard Bernstein,* 105.

p. 66 B. Bernstein, *Family Matters,* 141.

pp. 69–70 Ibid., 144.

p. 70 Secrest, 142.

p. 70 *New York Times,* November 15, 1943, 1A.

p. 70 L. Bernstein, *Findings,* 290.

p. 73 William Westbrook Burton, *Conversations About Bernstein* (New York: Oxford University Press, 1995), xvi.

pp. 73–74 Secrest, 107.

p. 76 Ibid., 141.

p. 76 Ibid; Ibid., 144.

p. 76 W. Burton, *Conversations,* 39.

p. 77 H. Burton, *Leonard Bernstein,* 156.

p. 79 Jean Shaw, interviewed by the author, 28 June 1999.

p. 79 B. Bernstein, *Family Matters,* 176.

p. 81 David Denby, "The Trouble With Lenny," *New Yorker,* August 17, 1998, 50.

p. 81 L. Bernstein, *Findings,* 154-155.

p. 83 H. Burton, *Leonard Bernstein,* 224.

p. 83 W. Burton, *Conversations,* 20.

p. 83 Ibid., 21.

p. 85 Denby, *New Yorker,* 48.

p. 86 Ibid., 47.

p. 87 Ibid., 44.

p. 89 Ibid., 47.

p. 90 W. Burton, *Conversations,* xxv.

pp. 90–91 H. Burton, *Leonard Bernstein,* 288.

p. 93 B. Bernstein, *Family Matters,* 195.

p. 94 H. Burton, *Leonard Bernstein,* 406.

p. 94 W. Burton, *Conversations,* xxix.

p. 94 Ibid.

p. 96 Jamie Bernstein Thomas, "The Media Maestro: Leonard Bernstein—Music Man," *Newsweek,* June 28, 1999, 56.

p. 96 H. Burton, *Leonard Bernstein,* 441.

p. 97 W. Burton, *Conversations,* xxx.

p. 97 Ibid.

p. 97 *Reaching for the Note.*

p. 97 Ibid.

p. 98 Schuyler Chapin, *Leonard Bernstein: Notes From A Friend* (New York: Walker, 1992), 132.

p. 99 H. Burton, *Leonard Bernstein,* 446–447.

p. 99 Ibid., 469.

p. 99 W. Burton, *Conversations,* xxxiii.

p. 99 Jean Shaw, interviewed by the author, 28 June 1999.

p. 101 Denby, *New Yorker,* 42.

pp. 103–104 H. Burton, *Leonard Bernstein,* 517.

p. 104 L. Bernstein, *Findings,* 154.

p. 104 *Reaching for the Note.*

p. 104 W. Burton, *Conversations,* xxxiv.

p. 105 *Reaching for the Note.*

p. 105 Chapin, 170–171.

Selected Bibliography

"Baton for Bernstein." *Time,* November 25, 1957, 55.

Bernstein, Burton. *Family Matters: Sam, Jennie, and the Kids.* New York: Summit Books, 1982.

Bernstein, Leonard. *Findings.* New York: Simon & Schuster, 1982. Reprint, New York: Anchor Books, 1993.

————. *The Infinite Variety of Music.* New York: Simon & Schuster, 1966. Reprint, New York: Anchor Books, 1993.

————. *The Joy of Music.* New York: Simon & Schuster, 1959. Reprint, New York: Anchor Books, 1994.

————. *Leonard Bernstein's Young People's Concerts.* Edited by Jack Gottlieb. New York: Simon & Schuster, 1962.

————. *The Unanswered Question.* Cambridge, MA: Harvard University Press/Cambridge Press, 1976.

Bernstein, Shirley. *Making Music: Leonard Bernstein.* Chicago: Encyclopedia Brittanica Press, 1963.

Burton, Humphrey. *Leonard Bernstein.* New York: Doubleday, 1994.

Burton, William Westbrook. *Conversations About Bernstein.* New York: Oxford University Press, 1995.

Chapin, Schuyler. *Leonard Bernstein: Notes From a Friend.* New York: Walker, 1992.

Denby, David. "The Trouble With Lenny." *New Yorker,* August 17, 1998, 42–53.

Gelb, Arthur, et al., eds. *Great Lives of the Twentieth Century.* New York: The New York Times Company, 1988.

Gottlieb, Jack, ed. *Bernstein on Broadway.* New York: Amberson, 1981.

Nies, Nancy S. "Founder's Day 1987: Honoring Helen Grace Coates and Leonard Bernstein." *Pine Manor College Bulletin,* Spring, 1987, 4–6.

Secrest, Meryle. *Leonard Bernstein: A Life.* New York: Alfred A. Knopf, Inc., 1994.

Thomas, Jamie Bernstein. "The Media Maestro: Leonard Bernstein—Music Man." *Newsweek,* June 28, 1999, 56.

"Wunderkind." *Time,* February 4, 1957, 70–75.

Further Reading

Briggs, John. *Leonard Bernstein: The Man, His Work, and His World.* Cleveland: World Publishing Co., 1961.

Deitch, Kenneth M., and Joanna B. Weisman. *Leonard Bernstein: America's Maestro.* Lowell, MA: Oxford University Press, 1990.

Fluegel, Jane, ed. *Bernstein Remembered.* New York: Carroll & Graf Publishers, Inc., 1991.

Gradenwitz, Peter. *Leonard Bernstein: The Infinite Variety of a Musician.* New York: St. Martin's Press, 1987.

Hurwitz, Johanna, and Sonia O. Lisker. *Leonard Bernstein: A Passion for Music.* Philadelphia: Jewish Publication Society, 1993.

Myers, Paul. *Leonard Bernstein.* London: Phaidon Press, 1998.

Peyser, Joan. *Bernstein: A Biography.* New York: Beech Tree Press, 1987.

Toby, Marlene. *Leonard Bernstein: All-American Musician.* Chicago: Children's Press, 1995.

Venzia, Mike. *Leonard Bernstein.* Chicago: Children's Press, 1997.

Selected Discography

Also Sprach Zarathustra/Don Juan/Till Eulenspiegel (Sony Classics)

Barber's Adagio & Other Romantic Favorites For Strings (Masterworks)

Bartok: Concerto for Orchestra (Sony Classical)

Beethoven: Missa Solemnis/Choral Fantasy/Mass No. 12, "Theresien Mass" (Sony Classical)

Beethoven: Piano Concertos Nos. 3 & 5, "Emperor" (Sony Classical)

Beethoven: Symphony No. 1 in C Major, Op. 21 (Sony Classical)

Beethoven: Symphony Nos. 2 & 7 (Sony Classical)

Beethoven: Symphony No. 3 in E-flat Major, Op. 55, "Eroica" (Sony Classical)

Beethoven: Symphonies Nos. 6 & 8 (Sony Classical)

Beethoven: Symphony No. 7 in A Major, Op. 92 (Sony Classical)

Beethoven: Violin Concerto (With Isaac Stern) (Sony Classical)

Berlioz: Harold in Italy, Op. 16 & La Mort De Cleopatre (Sony Classical)

Berlioz: Requiem/Mort de Cleopatre/Romeo and Juliet (Excerpts) (Sony Classical)

Berlioz: Symphonie Fantastique & Other Works (Sony Classical)

Bernstein: The Age of Anxiety and Other Works (Sony Classical)

Bernstein: Candide Overture Symphonic (Sony Classical)

Bernstein: Dybbuk (Sony Classical)

Bernstein: Prelude, Fugue and Riffs and Other Works (Sony Classical)

Bernstein: Trouble in Tahiti & Facsimile (Sony Classical)

Bernstein Conducts Bernstein (Sony Classical)

Bernstein Conducts Bernstein: Kaddish & Chichester Psalms (Sony Classical)

Bernstein Conducts Candide (Deutsche Grammophon)

Bernstein Conducts Gershwin and Grofé (Sony Classical)

Bernstein Conducts Tchaikovsky (Masterworks)

Bernstein Plays and Conducts Mozart (Sony Classical)

Brahms: Symphony No. 1, Serenade No. 2 (Sony Classical)

Brahms: Symphonies Nos. 2 & 3 (Sony Classical)

Chichester Psalms (Columbia)

Children's Classics (Columbia)

Children's Classics—Prokofiev: Peter & The Wolf, Complete Symphonies, Volume I, Nos. 1–3, Complete Symphonies, Volume II, Nos. 4–7 (Sony Classical)

Concert for Peace (Columbia)

Copland: Appalachian Spring & Other Works (Sony Classical)

Copland: Music for the Theater; Concerto for Piano & Orchestra (Sony Classical)

Copland: Rodeo (Four Dance Episodes)/Billy the Kid Ballet Suite (Sony Classical)

Copland: Symphony No. 3; Symphony for the Organ and Orchestra (Sony Classical)

Debussy: La Mer/Afternoon of a Faun/Two Nocturnes/Jeux (Sony Classical)

Fancy Free/On the Town (MCA)

Favorite Overtures (Columbia)

Gershwin: Rhapsody in Blue/An American in Paris [Masterworks] (Sony Classical)

Grofé: Grand Canyon Suite & Mississippi Suite (CBS Great Performances)

Haydn: The "London" Symphonies, Vol. 2 (Sony Classical)

Haydn: "Mass in Time of War"; "Nelson Mass"; Symphony No. 88 (Sony Classical)

Hindemith: Symphony in E-Flat Major (Sony Classical)

Ives: Symphony No. 2 & Symphony No. 3 (Sony Classical)

Ives: The Unanswered Question/Holidays (Sony Classical)

Mahler: Kindertotenlieder/Symphony No. 8, "Symphony of a Thousand" (Sony Classical)

Mahler: Symphony No. 1 in D Major, "Titan"/"Adagio" from Symphony No. 10 (Sony Classical)

Mahler: Symphony No. 2 in C Minor, "Resurrection" (Sony Classical)

Mahler: Symphony No. 3/Ruckert Lieder & Kindertotenlieder (Sony Classical)

Mahler: Symphony No. 4 in G Major (Sony Classical)

Mahler: Symphony No. 5 (Sony Classical)

Mahler: Symphony No. 7 (Sony Classical)

Mahler: Symphony No. 9 in D Major (Sony Classical)

Masterworks Heritage: Modern French Masterpieces (Sony Classical)

Mozart: Overture "Le Nozze Di Figaro," Symphonies No. 39 & 41 (Sony Classical)

Overtures (Columbia)

Shostakovich: Symphony Nos. 5 & 9 (Sony Classical)

Shostakovich: Symphony No. 14, Op. 135 (Sony Classical)

Stravinsky: The Rite of Spring; the Firebird Suite (Sony Classical)

Stravinsky: Le Sacre du Printemps/Petrushka (Sony Classical)

Symphonic Dances & Songs from West Side Story (Columbia)

Tchaikovsky: Ballet Music (Sony Classical)

Tchaikovsky: Symphony No. 3 in D Major/Op. 29/Polish/Romeo and Juliet (Sony Classical)

Tchaikovsky: Symphony No. 5/Marche Slave/1812 Overture (Sony Classical)

West Side Story (Pro Arte)

Wonderful Town (Angel)

Index

Other Titles in the Lerner Biographies Series

Photo Acknowledgments

About the Author

Caroline Evensen Lazo has written numerous biographies of men and women who have illuminated the world and enriched our lives. Her books include *Arthur Ashe* and *Alice Walker: Freedom Writer*—both Notable Social Studies Trade Books for Young People, selected by the National Council for Social Studies— and *Gloria Steinem: Feminist Extraordinaire.*

Ms. Lazo brings a personal touch to *Leonard Bernstein: In Love with Music.* She first met Bernstein when her sister, pianist Jean Shaw, was studying piano with Bernstein's teacher, Helen Coates. Lazo remembers the thrill of sitting in Bernstein's "house seats" during opening week of *West Side Story* on Broadway and celebrating other Bernstein events with her sister, to whom this book is dedicated.